POP PIANO HITS

SIMPLE ARRANGEMENTS FOR STUDENTS OF ALL AGES

I Don't Care, ME! & More Hot Singles

ISBN 978-1-5400-6113-3

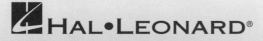

Visit Hal Leonard Online at
www.halleonard.com

Contact us:
Hal Leonard
7777 West Bluemound Road
Milwaukee, WI 53213
Email: info@halleonard.com

In Europe, contact:
Hal Leonard Europe Limited
42 Wigmore Street
Marylebone, London, W1U 2RN
Email: info@halleonardeurope.com

In Australia, contact:
Hal Leonard Australia Pty. Ltd.
4 Lentara Court
Cheltenham, Victoria, 3192 Australia
Email: info@halleonard.com.au

IF I CAN'T HAVE YOU

Words and Music by SHAWN MENDES,
TEDDY GEIGER, NATE MERCEREAU
and SCOTT HARRIS

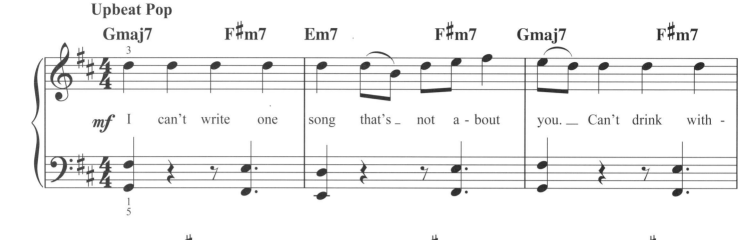

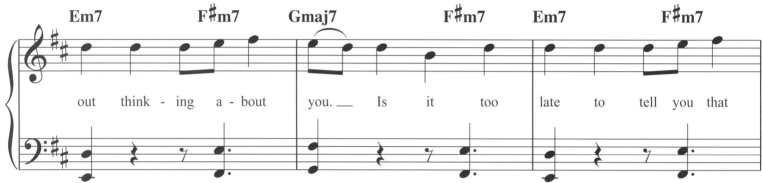

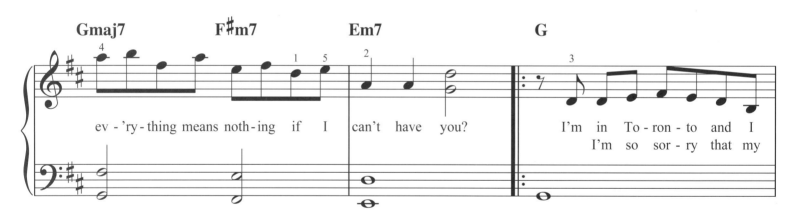

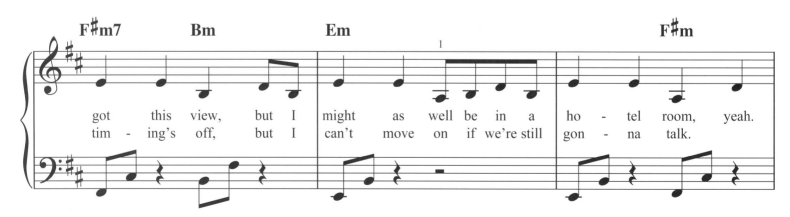

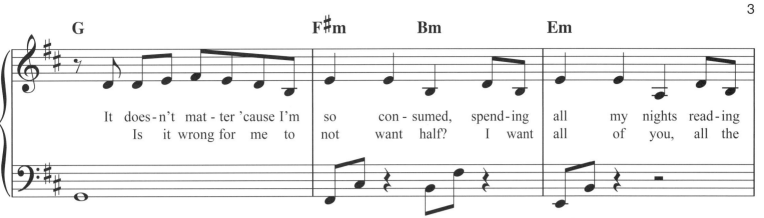

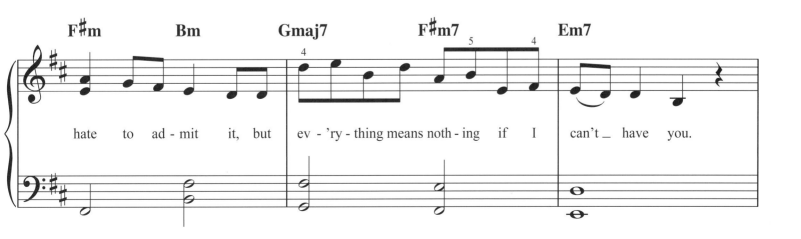

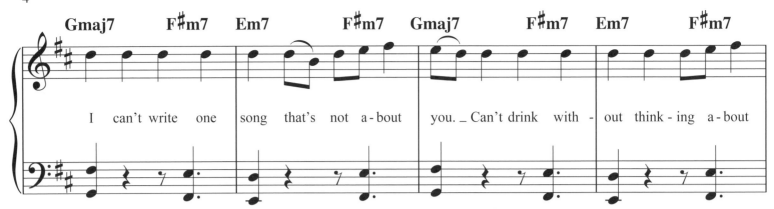

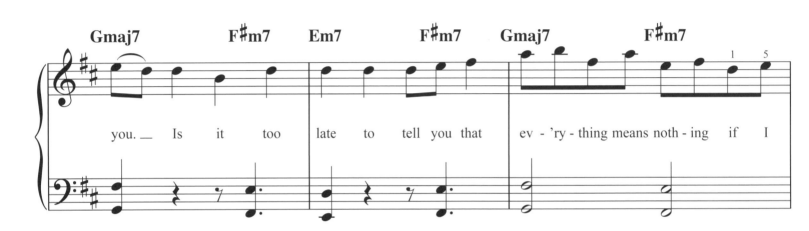

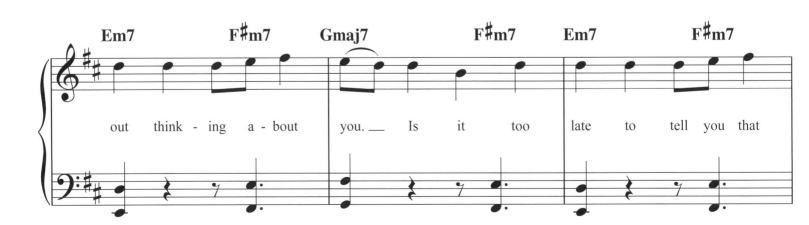

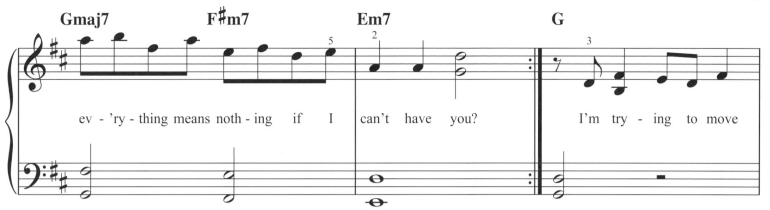

ev - 'ry - thing means noth - ing if I can't have you? I'm try - ing to move

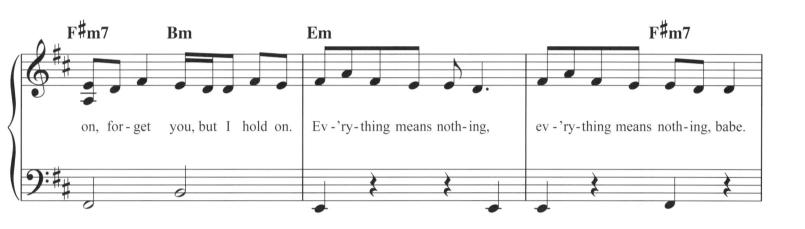

on, for - get you, but I hold on. Ev - 'ry - thing means noth - ing, ev - 'ry - thing means noth - ing, babe.

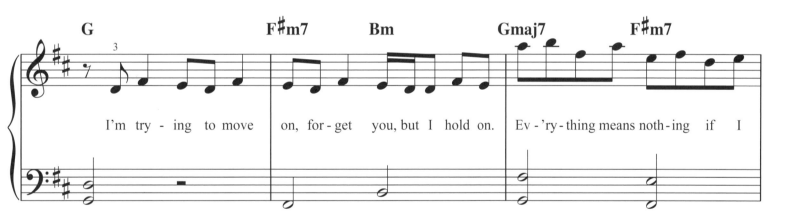

I'm try - ing to move on, for - get you, but I hold on. Ev - 'ry - thing means noth - ing if I

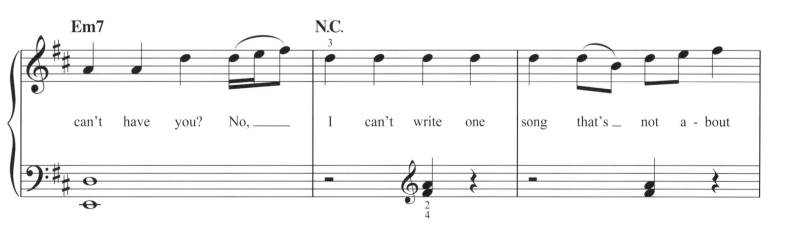

can't have you? No, ____ I can't write one song that's __ not a - bout

6

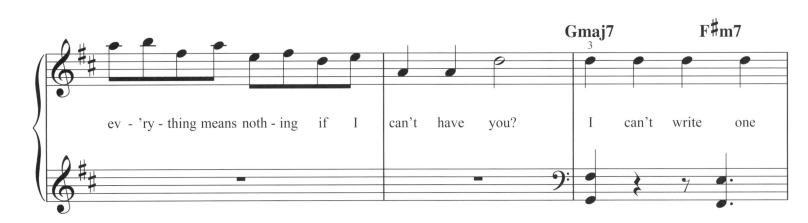

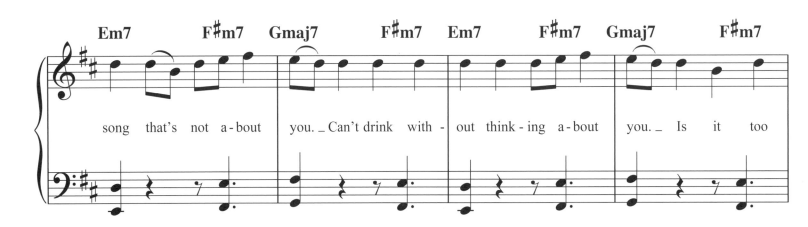

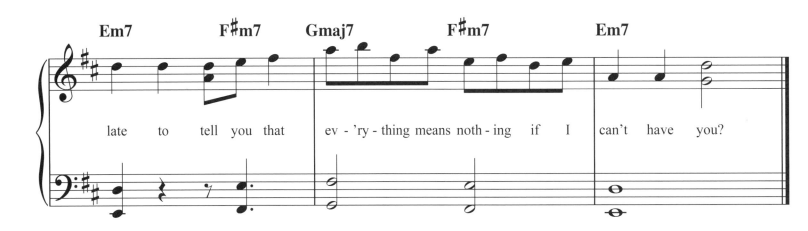

I DON'T CARE

Words and Music by ED SHEERAN,
JUSTIN BIEBER, FRED GIBSON,
JASON BOYD, MAX MARTIN
and SHELLBACK

Syncopated Pop

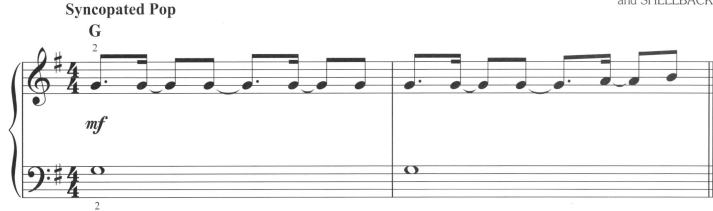

I'm at a par-ty I don't wan-na be at, and I don't ev-er wear a suit and tie, _

yeah. Won-der-ing if I can sneak out the back. No-bod-y's e-ven look-ing me in my _

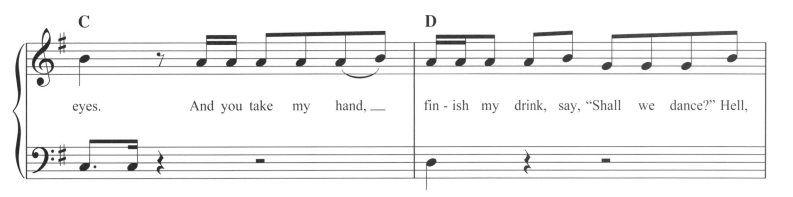

eyes. And you take my hand, _ fin-ish my drink, say, "Shall we dance?" Hell,

yeah. You know I love you; did I ev - er tell you? You make it bet - ter like that.

Don't think I fit in at this par - ty. ___ Ev - 'ry-one's got so much to
Don't think we fit in at this par - ty. ___ Ev - 'ry-one's got so much to

say, yeah. _ I al - ways feel like I'm no - bod - y, mm. _
say, yeah. _ When we walked in, I said, "I'm sor - ry," mm. _

Who wants to fit in an - y - way? 'Cause I don't care when I'm with my ba - by,
But now I think that we should stay.

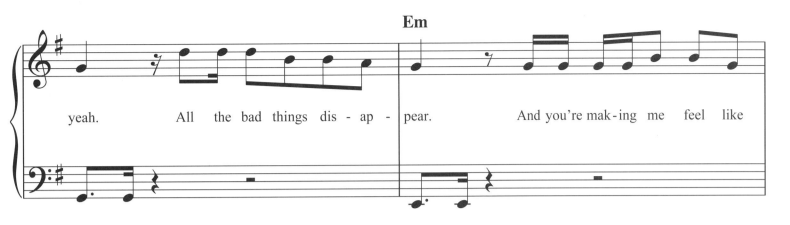

Em

yeah.   All   the bad things dis - ap - pear.   And you're mak-ing me   feel like

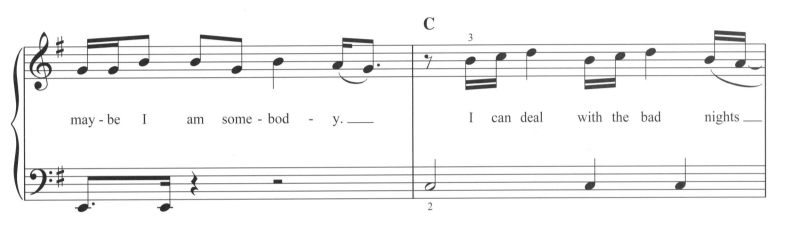

C

may - be   I   am some - bod - y. ___   I   can deal   with the bad   nights ___

D   G   8va

___   when I'm with my ba - by,   yeah.   Ooh ooh ooh ooh ooh __ ooh. __   'Cause I don't

care   as long   as you just hold me   near.   You can take me   an - y - where. __

And you're mak-ing me feel like I'm loved by some-bod - y. ___

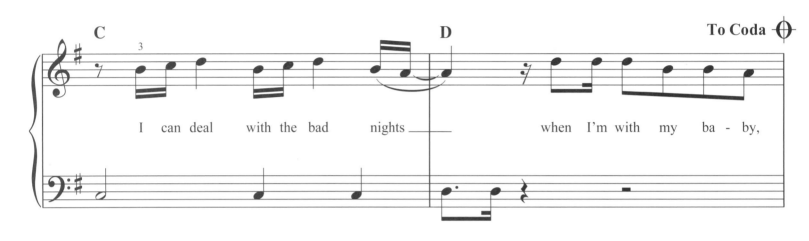

I can deal with the bad nights ___ when I'm with my ba - by,

yeah. Ooh ooh ooh ooh ooh ___ ooh. ___

We at a par-ty we don't wan-na be at, tryin' to talk, but we can't hear _ our-

selves. __ Read your lips, I'd rath-er kiss 'em right back. __ With all these peo-ple all a - round __ I'm crip -

- pled with __ anx-i - e-ty, ___ but I'm told ___ it's where __ we're s'posed __ to be. __ You know

D.S. al Coda

what? __ It's kind of cra-zy 'cause I real-ly don't mind ____ when __ you make it bet-ter like that.

CODA

yeah. __ Ooh ooh ooh ooh ooh __ ooh. ___ No. _____

care   when I'm with my ba - by,   yeah.   All the bad things dis - ap -
care   as long as you just hold me   near.   You can take me an - y -

pear.   And you're mak-ing me feel like | may-be I am some-bod - y. __
where.   And you're mak-ing me feel like | I'm loved by some-bod - y. __

I can deal with the bad nights __

___   when I'm with my ba - by, yeah.   Ooh ooh ooh ooh ooh __ ooh. __

1.

'Cause I don't

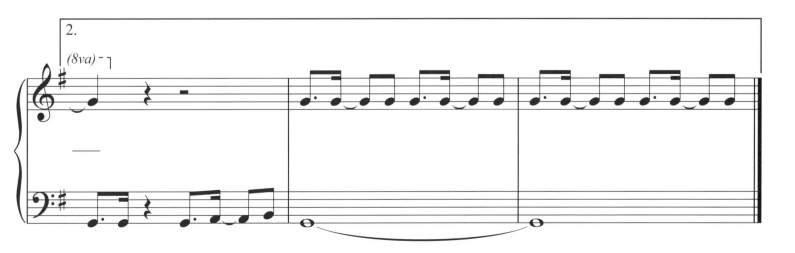

2.

ME!

Words and Music by TAYLOR SWIFT,
JOEL LITTLE and BRENDON URIE

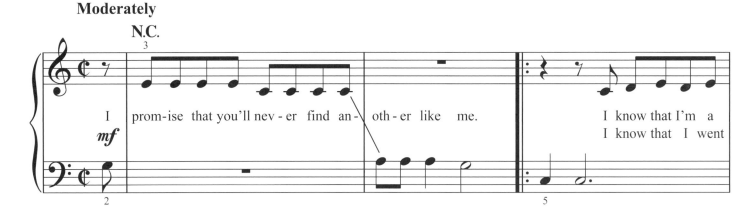

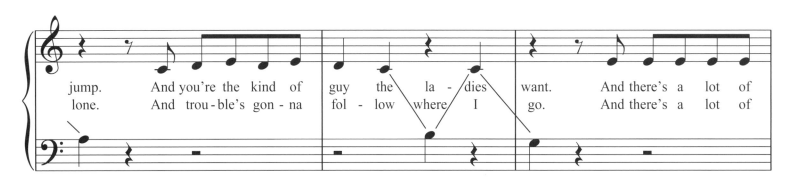

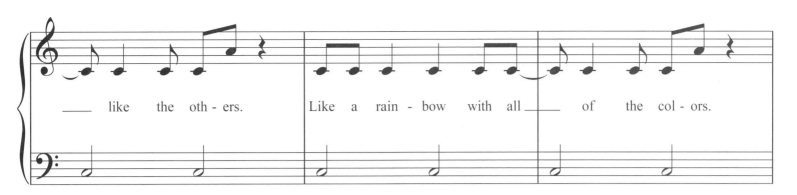

_____ like the oth - ers. Like a rain - bow with all _____ of the col - ors.

N.C.

Ba - by doll, when it comes _____ to a lov - er, I prom - ise that you'll nev - er find an -

C

Am

oth - er like me, ee ee. Ooh, ooh, ooh. _____

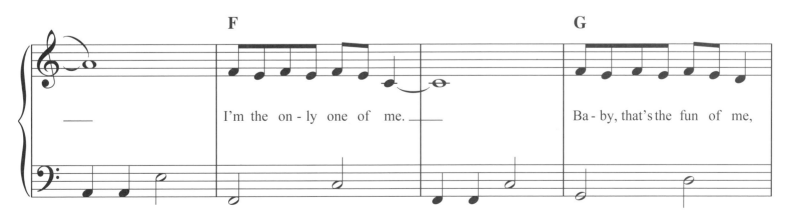

F

G

_____ I'm the on - ly one of me. _____ Ba - by, that's the fun of me,

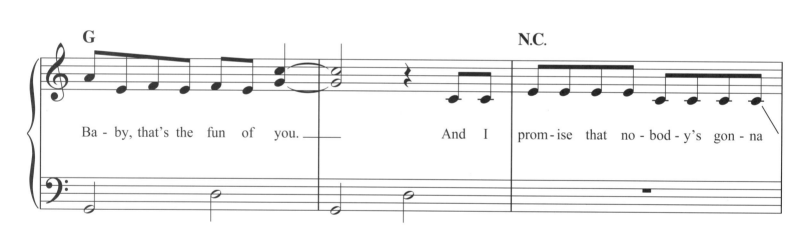

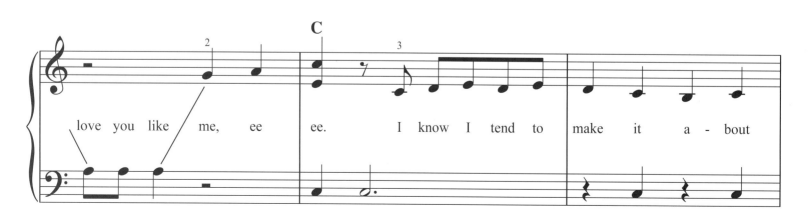

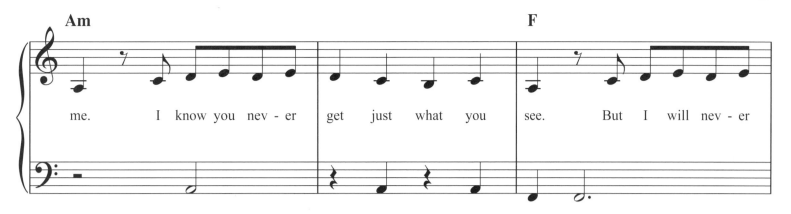

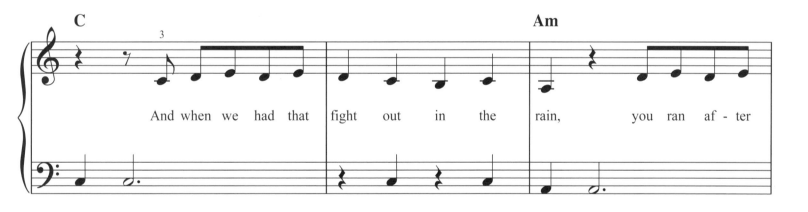

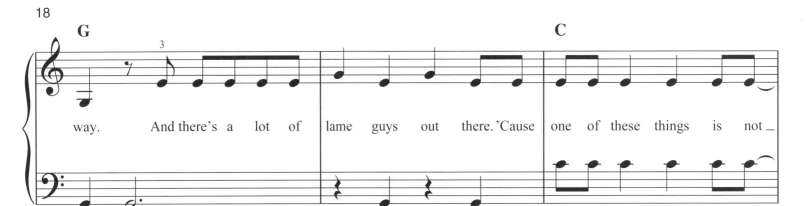

G

way. And there's a lot of lame guys out there. 'Cause **C** one of these things is not___

___ like the oth-ers. Liv-ing in win-ter, I___ am your sum-mer.

N.C.

Ba-by doll, when it comes___ to a lov-er, I prom-ise that you'll nev-er find an-

𝄋 C

oth-er like me, ee ee. **Am** Ooh, ooh, ooh.___

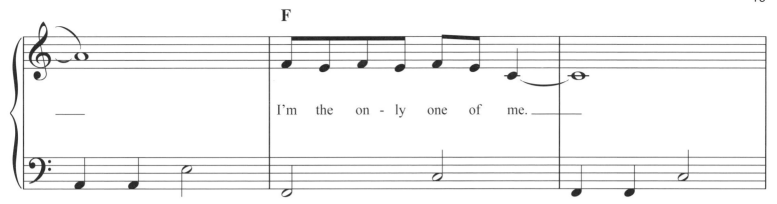

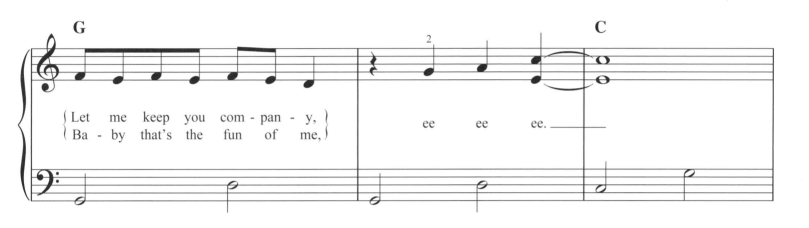

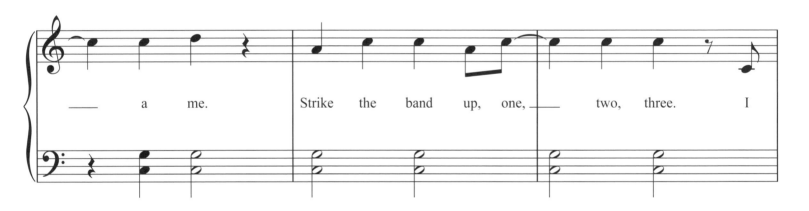

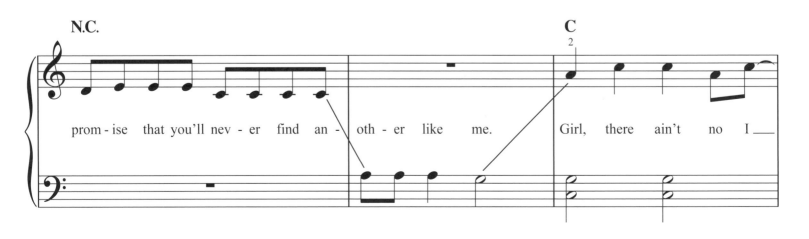

in team. But you know there is ___ a me. And you can't spell awe - some with-

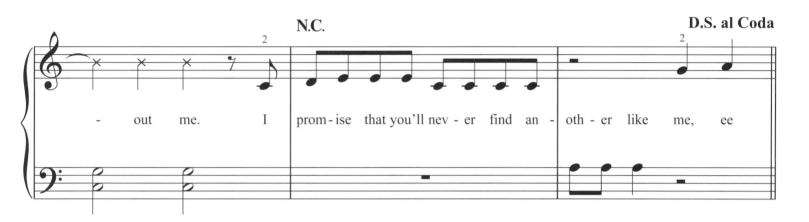

N.C. **D.S. al Coda**

- out me. I prom - ise that you'll nev - er find an - oth - er like me, ee

CODA **C**

love you like me. Girl, there ain't no I___ in team.

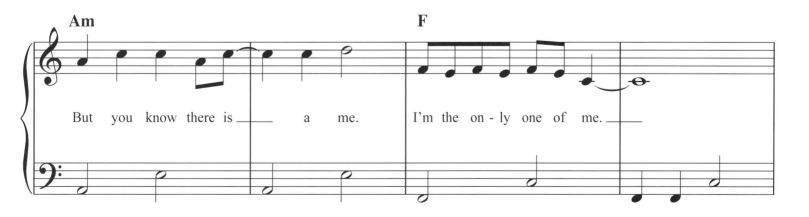

Am **F**

But you know there is___ a me. I'm the on - ly one of me.

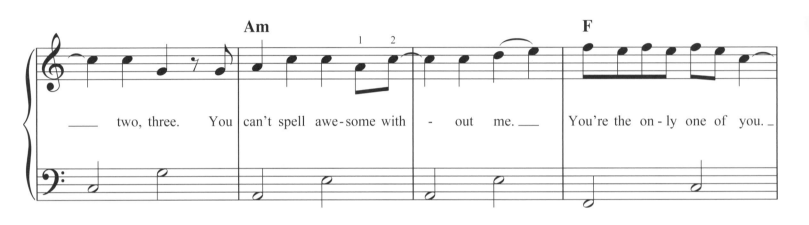

RAINBOW

Words and Music by KACEY MUSGRAVES,
SHANE McANALLY and NATALIE HEMBY

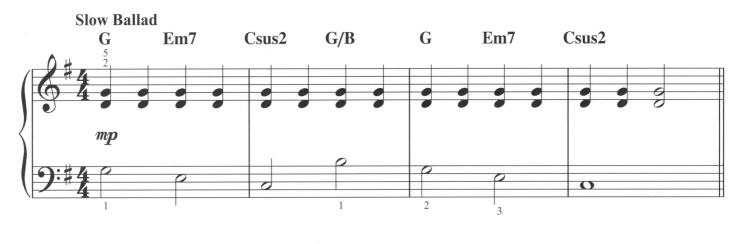

When it rains, — it pours, — but you did-n't e - ven no - tice it ain't

rain - ing an - y - more. — It's hard to breathe when all — you know is the

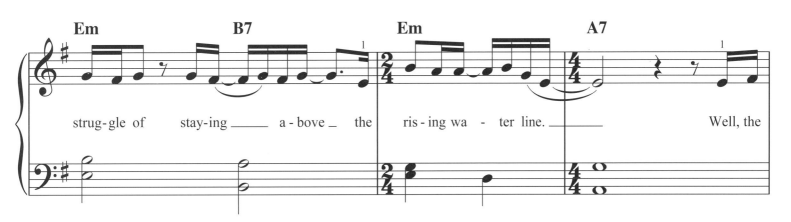

strug-gle of stay-ing —— a - bove — the ris-ing wa - ter line. —— Well, the

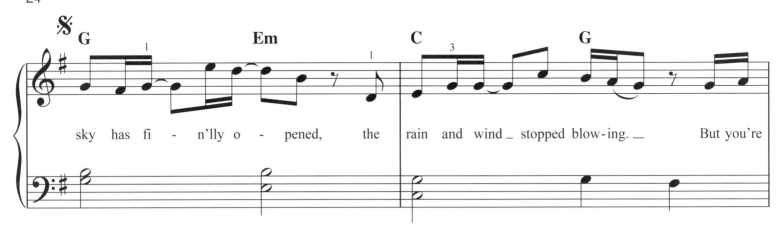

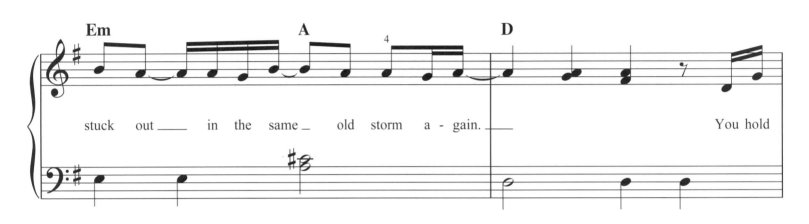

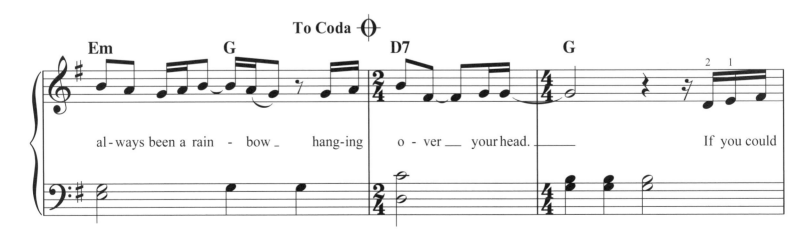

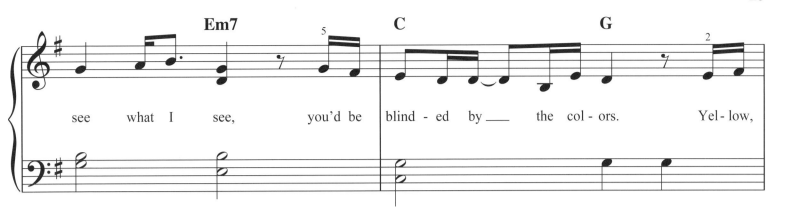

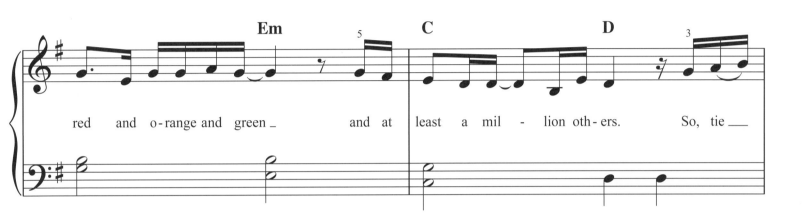

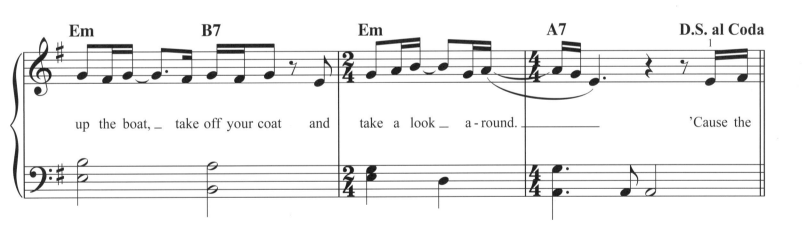

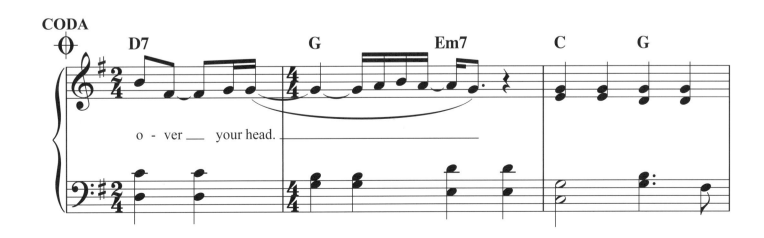

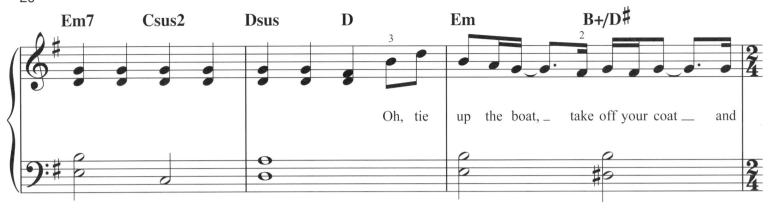

Oh, tie up the boat, __ take off your coat __ and

take a look __ a - round. _____ Ev-'ry-thing is al - right now. 'Cause the

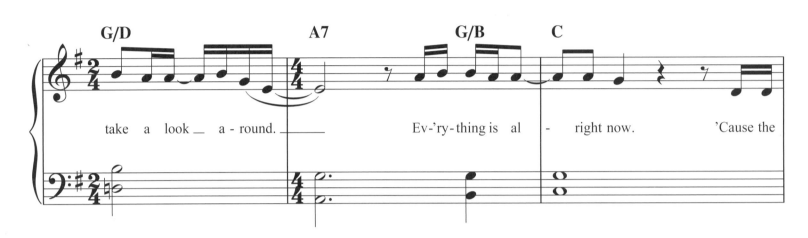

sky has fi - n'lly o - pened, the rain and wind __ stopped blow - ing. But you're

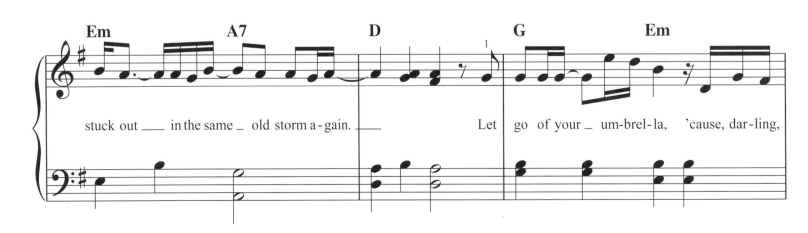

stuck out ___ in the same __ old storm a - gain. ___ Let go of your __ um-brel-la, 'cause, dar-ling,

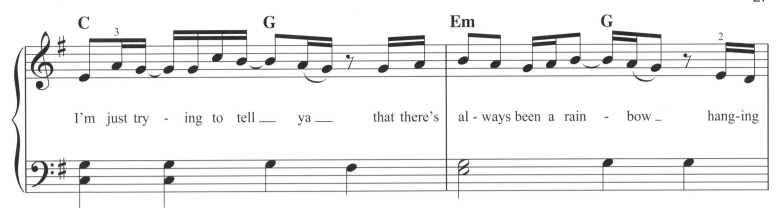

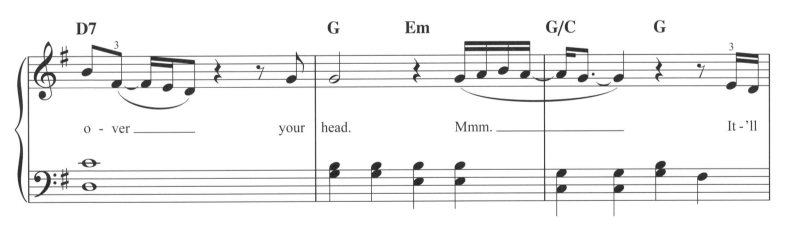

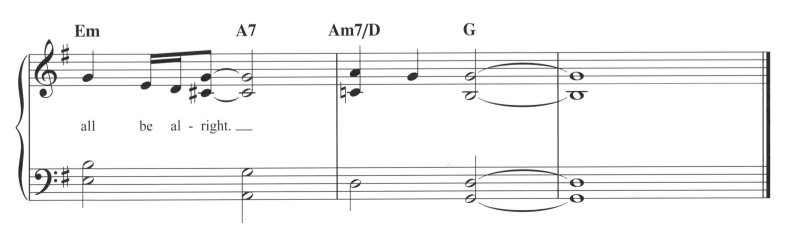

SOMEONE YOU LOVED

Words and Music by LEWIS CAPALDI,
BENJAMIN KOHN, PETER KELLEHER
THOMAS BARNES and SAMUEL ROMAN

Moderate Ballad

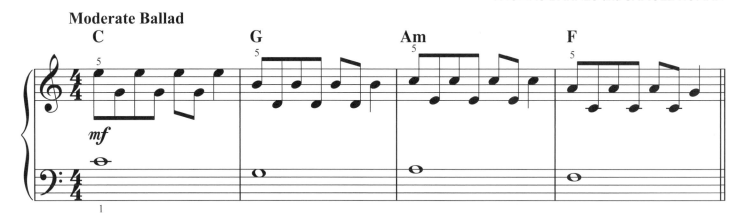

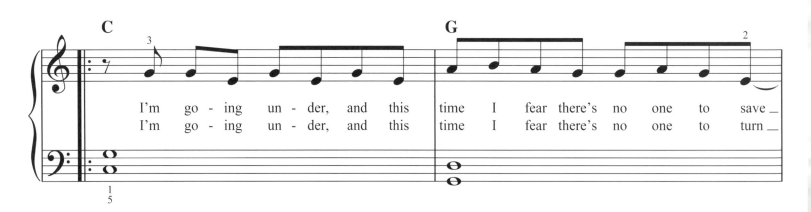

I'm go-ing un-der, and this time I fear there's no one to save ___
I'm go-ing un-der, and this time I fear there's no one to turn ___

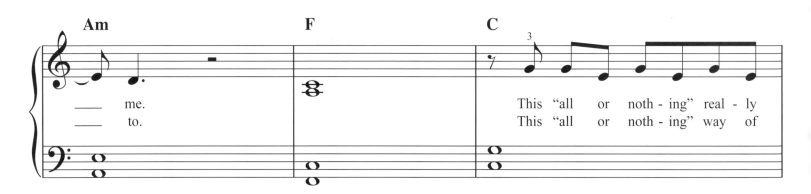

___ me. This "all or noth-ing" real-ly
___ to. This "all or noth-ing" way of

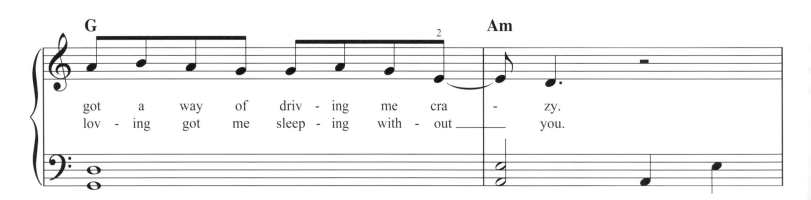

got a way of driv-ing me cra - zy.
lov-ing got me sleep-ing with-out ___ you.

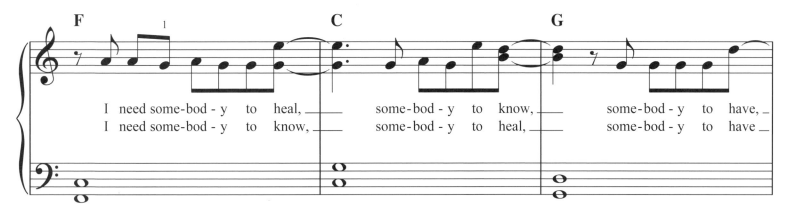

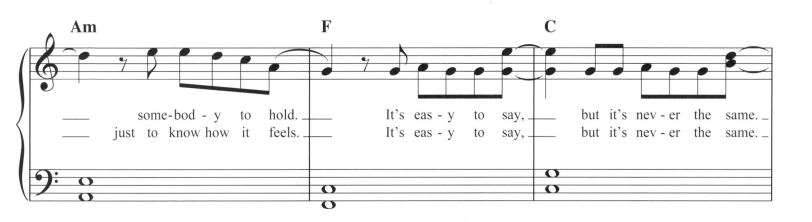

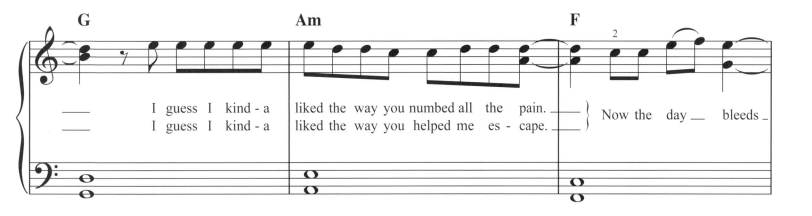

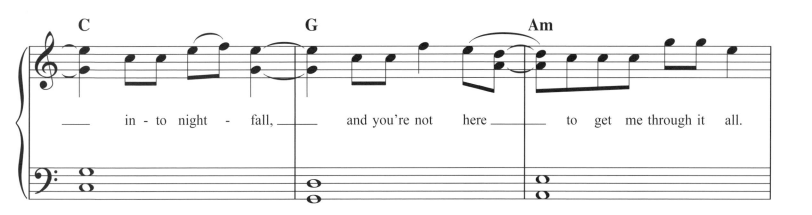

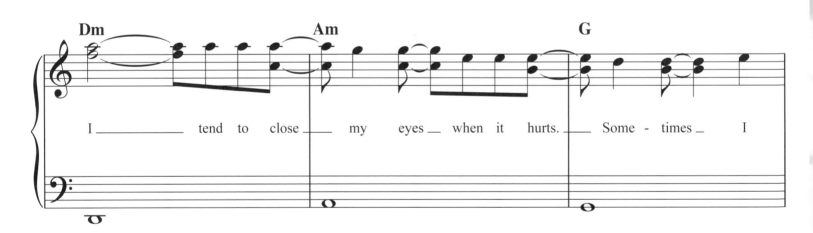

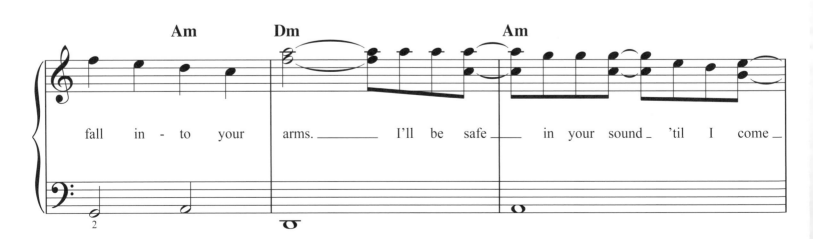

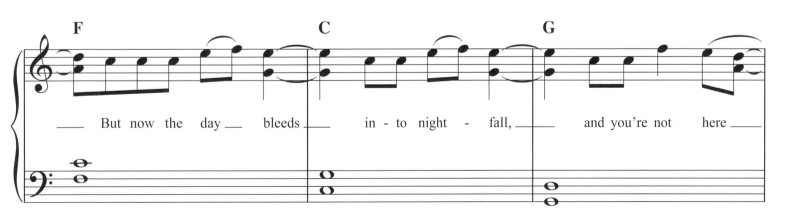

Am _____ to get me through it all. **F** I let my guard down, _____ and then you pulled the **C** rug. _____

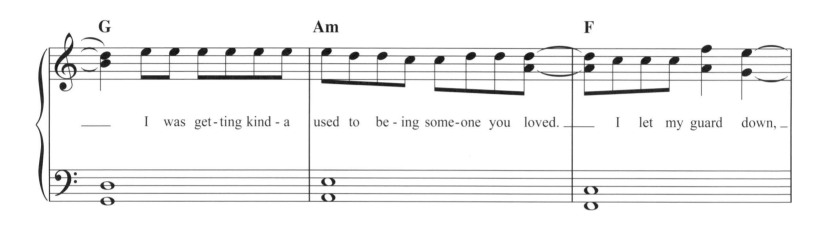

G _____ I was get-ting kind - a **Am** used to be - ing some-one you loved. _____ I let my guard **F** down, _____

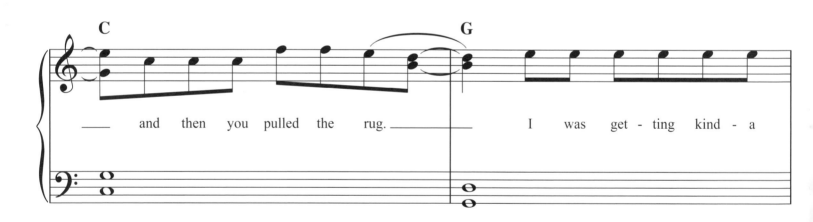

C _____ and then you pulled the rug. _____ **G** I was get - ting kind - a

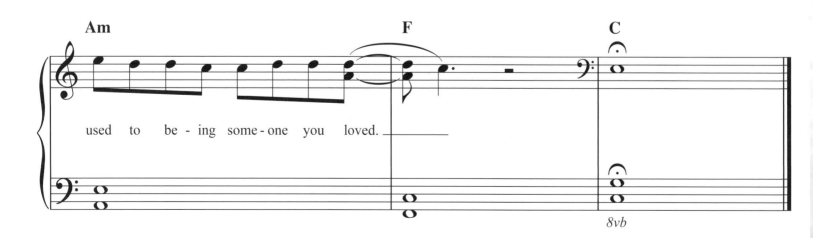

Am used to be - ing some-one you loved. _____ **F** **C**

8vb